The Shakespeare Library

Romeo & Juliet

WENDY GREENHILL

HEAD OF EDUCATION,
ROYAL SHAKESPEARE COMPANY

Heinemann

Heinemann Library,
an imprint of Heinemann Publishers (Oxford) Ltd,
Halley Court, Jordan Hill, Oxford, England, OX2 8EJ.

OXFORD LONDON EDINBURGH MADRID PARIS
ATHENS BOLOGNA MELBOURNE SYDNEY
AUCKLAND SINGAPORE TOKYO IBADAN
NAIROBI GABORONE HARARE PORTSMOUTH NH (USA)

First published 1995
95 96 97 10 9 8 7 6 5 4 3 2 1

British Library Cataloguing in Publication Data
Greenhill, Wendy
'Romeo and Juliet'. – (Shakespeare Library)
I. Title II. Series
822.33

ISBN 0 431 07523 9

Designed by Green Door Design Ltd
Printed and bound in Hong Kong

Acknowledgements
The author and publishers would like to thank the following for
permission to reproduce photographs:

The British Library, page 4;
Donald Cooper, pages 6, 7, 8, 9, 11, 12, 13, 15, 17, 25, 27, 30, 31;
E. T. Archive, page 20;
Mander and Mitchenson Theatre Collection, pages 10, 22, 28;
The Illustrated London News Picture Library, page 21;
Shakespeare Centre Library/Angus McBean, page 23;
Shakespeare Centre Library/Joe Cocks Studio Collection, pages 24, 29;
University of Bristol Theatre Collection, page 26

Names in **bold** in the text are the characters in the play.

The cover shows a scene taken from the 1976 production performed
at The Other Place, Stratford upon Avon.

CONTENTS

THE SOURCES OF ROMEO AND JULIET

By 1594 or 1595 when *Romeo and Juliet* was most probably written, Shakespeare had already begun to make his mark in the London theatre. Since about 1590 he had been working there as an actor and playwright. Back home in Stratford upon Avon he had left behind a wife, whom he had married when he was eighteen, and three children. His eldest child, Susannah, was thirteen, around the age of Juliet. Shakespeare himself was 30 years old. He was an experienced man, poised for success in what was still an exciting new form of entertainment: the theatre.

Shakespeare had a shrewd understanding of the subjects which would be popular with audiences, and the theme of tragic young love was no exception. A version of *Romeo and Juliet*, printed and sold in London in 1599, was described as 'an excellent and lamentable tragedy…'. *Romeo and Juliet* was a success right from the start.

The story of Romeo and Juliet was well known in several forms before Shakespeare made it his own. There had been poems, plays and stories in Italian and French. In 1567, borrowing from these European originals, William Painter had included 'The goodly history of Rhomeo and Julietta' in a volume of short stories. Even earlier, in 1562, another writer, Arthur Brooke, had turned the story into a long poem, 'The Tragical History of Romeus and Juliet'. There are many similarities between Brooke's poem and Shakespeare's play, and it is likely that Shakespeare had the poem in front of him as he wrote.

THE
MOST EX-
cellent and lamentable
Tragedie, of Romeo
and Iuliet.

Newly corrected, augmented, and
amended:

As it hath bene sundry times publiquely acted, by the
right Honourable the Lord Chamberlaine
his Seruants.

LONDON
Printed by Thomas Creede, for Cuthbert Burby, and are to
be sold at his shop neare the Exchange.
1599.

The 1599 edition of Shakespeare's *Romeo and Juliet*. A 'tragedie' of young love was sure to be popular.

This illustration, from 1616, shows a dual.

IMPROVING ON THE ORIGINALS

It was quite normal for Elizabethan playwrights to use existing stories as the basis for their plays. Shakespeare was a master at choosing the most interesting ideas and developing them into something more complex than the originals. In *Romeo and Juliet* we find a wider range of attitudes to love than in any of the stories on which it was based. **Mercutio** is a character who takes one extreme view. For him love means sex. He is full of brutal bravado. He mocks pretensions to romantic love and so is a marked contrast to **Romeo**. But he is mentioned in only one line of Brooke's poem.

It has to be said, in fact, that Brooke's poem is rather dull. But Shakespeare turns it into a story of great contrasts. Right from the start there is a sense of dreadful fate: we know that the lovers are doomed. But along the way we have music, dancing, comedy, sword fights and wit. The play is a wonderful piece of theatre, full of action and energy.

Shakespeare's use of language, too, is much more· interesting. The contrasts in the play are expressed in many different styles. These range from formal poetry to witty puns, from the angry outbursts of Juliet's father to the passionate idealism of the lovers. We feel the atmosphere of the play through its language.

THE STAR-CROSSED LOVERS

The opening **Chorus** refers to **Romeo** and **Juliet** as 'A pair of star-crossed lovers'. This famous description conveys the brilliant intensity of their love as well as the tragedy of their deaths. They fall in love at first sight and within a day they are married. **Friar Laurence** warns that love of such intensity cannot last long:

'These violent delights have violent ends'.

The two lovers often talk of each other as light or stars or sun. Romeo calls Juliet 'the sun', 'bright angel', 'my soul'. For her, he is like the stars:

'Come, loving, black-browed night.

Give me my Romeo. And when I shall die,

Take him and cut him out in little stars,

And he will make the face of heaven so fine

That all the world will be in love with night.'

(Act 3, Scene 2, lines 20–24)

This is one of several moments when Juliet has a premonition of death. Bright light is the symbol of their love but they are also aware that light is overshadowed by darkness and that eternal darkness means death. As dawn breaks after their wedding night and Romeo must leave for Mantua, they say:

'JULIET: O, now be gone! More light and light it grows.

ROMEO: More light and light: more dark and dark our woes.'

Judy Buxton as Juliet and Trevor Baxter as Capulet in Ron Daniel's 1980 RSC production.

A Doomed Love

The sense that their lives and love are doomed grows bit by bit but, at the beginning of the play, both young people seem fortunate. Romeo's mother cares about him and is pleased he wasn't involved in the recent outbreak of violence between the families. Juliet's father seems loving and protective towards her, trying to persuade **Paris** that she is too young to marry. Juliet's house comes to life in the party her father has enjoyed organizing and when **Tybalt** recognizes Romeo, **Capulet** won't have him turned out because he is 'a virtuous and well-governed youth', not a trouble-maker.

But such affection and good sense is fragile and short-lived; and the reality of Juliet's life, and quickly Romeo's too, is lonely and insecure. No other characters, least of all their parents, have anything like the honesty and faithfulness of the lovers. **Lady Capulet** was married young herself, is only 28 now, and has a cool relationship with both her husband and daughter. When Juliet appeals to her mother for help,

> **'O sweet mother, cast me not away!'**

There is no sympathy at all in the reply:

> **'Talk not to me, for I'll not speak a word.**
>
> **Do as thou wilt, for I have done with thee.'**

When even the **Nurse** thinks that Juliet should cut her losses, forget Romeo and marry Paris, Juliet grows up in a moment: she must be responsible for her own decisions. She is prepared to die if all other plans fail.

Juliet's appeals for her parents' understanding are met with coolness. Düsseldorfer Schauspielhaus, 1994.

VICTIMS OF CHANCE?

You could say that **Romeo** and **Juliet** die because of terrible bad luck. **Friar Laurence** is their counsellor and friend but in the end they are alone: Romeo to endure banishment and Juliet to face waking up in a tomb. They cannot even keep in contact with one another. Such total loneliness makes them very vulnerable. When things go horribly wrong and Romeo believes that Juliet is really dead, the Friar tries to save the situation – but he is too late.

Watching the play on stage we feel that the story could work out differently. There are so many 'if onlys': if only **Mercutio** had not been killed; if only Friar Laurence had used a better messenger; if only Juliet had woken up five minutes earlier. Our sense of mis-chance – bad luck – is very strong. In a good performance of the play it is the painful sense of 'if only' which makes us feel that this is, indeed, a tragic love story.

The famous balcony scene, where Romeo and Juliet vow true love and devotion to each other. This scene is from Terry Hands' 1989 production.

A TRAGEDY OF TWO FAMILIES

Romeo and Juliet have been born into a world of violence and hate. As the only children of two powerful, constantly feuding families, they are caught up in a whirlwind of anger, insults, brawling and death. New acts of violence keep them apart, even after they have declared their love. Their wretchedness lies in this isolation. What chance has a secret love set against organized hate? Romeo and Juliet are powerless. They are out-numbered, out-manoeuvred and 'out-gunned'.

But in the end the play is a tragedy not just of two young lovers but also of two great families. The bitter outcome of the years of feuding is that the **Montagues** and **Capulets** alike lose their only child. The families are as doomed as Romeo and Juliet. In the final scene they agree to end the violence and erect statues in memory of the dead lovers, but there is still a sense of shocking and irretrievable waste. As the Prince says:

'A glooming peace this morning with it brings:
The sun for sorrow will not show his head...

For never was a story of more woe
Than this of Juliet and her Romeo.'

Romeo grieves Juliet's 'death'. The audience feels both sad and anxious, knowing his mistaken belief will lead to tragedy. This scene is from the 1992 Leveaux production by the RSC.

THE CHARACTERS IN THE PLAY

ESCALUS Prince of Verona

MERCUTIO related to the Prince and a friend of Romeo

PARIS a young nobleman, related to the Prince and Mercutio. In love with Juliet

SERVANT to COUNT PARIS

MONTAGUE the head of a family of Verona, feuding with the Capulets

LADY MONTAGUE his wife

ROMEO their only child

BENVOLIO Romeo's cousin and friend

ABRAHAM Montague's servant

BALTHASAR Romeo's servant

CAPULET the head of a family of Verona, feuding with the Montagues

LADY CAPULET his wife

JULIET their only child

TYBALT Juliet's cousin

An OLD MAN of the Capulet family

NURSE to Juliet

PETER a servant of the Capulet family

Romeo tries to calm things down between his friend Mercutio and the Capulet Tybalt. This scene is from Gielgud's production in 1935.

Men of the Capulet household:
SAMPSON
GREGORY
ANTHONY
POTPAN
A CLOWN
A SERVANT

FRIAR LAURENCE a Franciscan; Romeo's friend and Juliet's helper

FRIAR JOHN a Franciscan; Friar Laurence sends him to Mantua with a letter for Romeo

AN APOTHECARY living in Mantua; he supplies Romeo with poison.

Three Musicians:

Simon Catling

Hugh Rebeck

James Soundpost

Members of the watch, citizens of Verona, dancers, torchbearers, pages and servants

The **Chorus** who opens the play. A character who plays no part in the story but comments on it.

Before the tragedy unfolds – the happy affection between Juliet and the Nurse. This scene is taken from Leveaux's 1992 production by the RSC.

What Happens in the Play

The Quarrel

The young men of the Montague and Capulet families are at it again: their long-standing feud has boiled over and they are brawling in the street. **Escalus**, Prince of Verona, comes to break it up and orders a ban on fighting in the streets: if they cannot control themselves he must do it for them. **Romeo** hasn't been involved this time: he's feeling miserable because he's in love with Rosaline, but she doesn't love him. His cousin **Benvolio** tells him to find another girl.

A Question of Marriage

Meanwhile in the Capulet's house, the Count **Paris** is asking to marry **Juliet**. He tells her father that at fourteen she is not too young. **Capulet** would prefer him to wait for two years but eventually tells

Paris to speak to **Juliet**. If she consents then he will give his permission. Capulet invites Paris to a party he is giving that night: it will be a chance for him to meet Juliet.

BEFORE THE PARTY

Romeo and Benvolio hear about Capulet's party, and that Rosaline will be there. They decide to gatecrash. **Lady Capulet** tells Juliet about Count Paris. Both she and Juliet's **Nurse** encourage her to watch him at the party: he would be a fine catch, if she could love him as a husband.

THE PARTY

The party is in full swing when the Montagues arrive, wearing masks so they won't be recognized. During a dance Romeo sees a girl. At once Rosaline is forgotten. It is love at first sight.

'Did my heart love till now?
Foreswear it, sight!

For I ne'er saw beauty till this
night.'

Tybalt, Juliet's cousin, recognizes Romeo as a Montague and wants to throw him out; Capulet, however, insists that the party should not be spoiled: he's heard good things about Romeo, who in any case isn't making trouble. But Tybalt is furious and is determined to get his own back on the Montagues later. Romeo manages to have a few moments alone with Juliet. He kisses her. The Nurse interrupts to call Juliet to her mother and Romeo realizes she's a Capulet, and the daughter of the house. He leaves at once. The Nurse tells Juliet about Romeo and she realizes that she's in an impossible position: she loves a family enemy.

Capulet's party in full swing. This scene is from the 1994 production at the Schauspielhaus in Dusseldorf.

THE BALCONY SCENE

Romeo's friends have lost him in the rush to get away from the party unharmed. They think he must be nearby so they tease him about Rosaline. He doesn't answer and they leave.

Romeo comes out of hiding and sees Juliet standing at her window. Coming nearer he hears her speaking: she is talking about him and how she loves him. They vow true love and devotion to each other.

Juliet suggests that they marry in secret: their two families hate each other too much to allow them to make their love public. She will send a message to Romeo telling him where and when they can meet for the ceremony.

The Nurse calls Juliet inside and reluctantly she goes. Romeo leaves to visit his friend **Friar Laurence** for advice and help.

FRIAR LAURENCE'S CELL

Romeo tells the Friar how deeply he is in love with Juliet. Friar Laurence, remembering his young friend's infatuation with Rosaline (now so easily displaced) wants more convincing. But he is hopeful that, if it is true love, then a marriage might heal the old feud between the families.

THE GO-BETWEEN

The Nurse is sent to find Romeo. She warns him not to deceive Juliet but Romeo convinces her of his seriousness. She agrees to help Juliet find a way of going to Friar Laurence's cell that afternoon. It is there that the two lovers will be married. Juliet is impatient for news when the Nurse returns but eventually learns of Romeo's plan. While she prepares for the visit to Friar Laurence for the marriage ceremony the Nurse goes to find the ladder which will help Romeo climb up to Juliet's bedroom that night.

THE MARRIAGE CEREMONY

Juliet joins Romeo at Friar Laurence's cell and he takes them off to be married.

Sean Bean as Romeo and Niamh Cusack as Juliet in Bogdanov's production by the RSC in 1986. This scene shows Friar Laurence uniting Romeo and Juliet in marriage.

A FIGHT

Benvolio and **Mercutio** meet Tybalt and other Capulets. Tybalt is still spoiling for a fight with Romeo after the incident at the Capulet party but Romeo, when he arrives, refuses to fight. He tries to calm things down by reminding everyone of the Prince's order. But Mercutio will not be stopped and takes up Tybalt's challenge. Romeo steps between the two friends which results in a sword being thrust into Mercutio's body. Mercutio, badly wounded, blames Romeo for interfering, and both families for the feud. He dies. When Tybalt comes back Romeo fights and kills him. Benvolio tells Romeo that Romeo will be held responsible if the Prince hears about the fight.

Almost at once the Prince arrives with the Montagues and the Capulets. Benvolio tells them what happened and Lady Capulet demands that Romeo be executed. The Prince, however, seeing that Romeo was avenging the death of Mercutio orders that he be banished. Romeo must leave Verona.

BANISHMENT

Juliet is waiting impatiently for night when Romeo will come to her. The Nurse gives her the news of Tybalt's death and Romeo's punishment; Juliet is distraught. Meanwhile, Friar Laurence is bringing Romeo news of his banishment. Romeo cannot bear the thought of leaving Juliet. The Nurse now arrives to tell Romeo of Juliet's grief. Only Friar Laurence seems able to think straight and he tells Romeo to visit that night as planned. But he must leave before dawn and go to Mantua, a distant city. Friar Laurence will try to reconcile the Montagues and Capulets with news of their children's marriage. When he is successful, then Romeo can come back to be with Juliet.

A MARRIAGE IS ARRANGED

Count Paris, however, is still determined to marry Juliet. Her parents, numbed by the shock of Tybalt's death, and without consulting her, agree: Juliet and Paris will marry in three days' time.

THE LOVERS PART

Romeo and Juliet have spent their wedding night together. Dawn is breaking as Romeo leaves. Looking down on him from her balcony Juliet imagines him in a tomb.

Juliet's mother now arrives to tell Juliet of her marriage to Paris. Shocked, Juliet answers plainly: no. She repeats this to her father who loses his temper and threatens to disown her if she disobeys. Neither her father nor her mother will listen to her and Juliet turns to the Nurse for help, but even she doesn't understand how much Juliet is in love. She tells Juliet to forget Romeo: he's banished and may never return. Juliet seems to agree and goes to Friar Laurence's cell to pray, she says, for forgiveness.

Romeo fights Tybalt, and avenges the death of Mercutio. This is taken from the 1973 production at the RST.

AT FRIAR LAURENCE'S CELL

Paris is asking the Friar to be ready to marry them when Juliet arrives. Once alone with the Friar she tells him she will kill herself rather than be unfaithful to Romeo. Friar Laurence, understanding her strength, outlines a daring plan. She is to go home and agree to marry Paris. The next night she must drink a special potion before going to sleep: it will make her appear to be dead. Her parents will bury her in the family tomb. Meanwhile Friar Laurence will tell Romeo what is happening. Romeo will come back, go to the tomb, wake Juliet and they will be reunited. Juliet agrees.

PREPARING FOR A WEDDING – AND A DEATH

As the Capulets prepare the marriage feast Juliet goes to her room. She is afraid of waking up in the tomb before Romeo arrives and afraid that the potion won't work. In that case she will stab herself to death rather than marry Paris. Finally, thinking of Romeo, she drinks the potion.

THE DEATH DISCOVERED

Juliet is found 'dead' on her wedding morning. Her parents, the Nurse and Paris are overcome by grief, so the Friar is able to take charge. She is buried without delay in the family tomb.

THE PLAN GOES WRONG

Romeo's servant, **Balthasar**, returns to Mantua from Verona with tragic news. He has seen Juliet lowered into the tomb. Convinced she is dead, Romeo finds poison and goes back to Verona to kill himself at Juliet's grave.

Friar Laurence has sent Friar John with a letter to Romeo in which the apparent death of Juliet is explained. But Friar John is not allowed into Mantua: the authorities think he is carrying the plague. When Friar Laurence realizes that Romeo has not been given the message he goes himself to Juliet's tomb. He will be there when she wakes and hide her in his cell until Romeo can be brought to Verona.

AT JULIET'S GRAVE

Paris and his servant come to the tomb. Hearing someone, Paris hides. It is Romeo and Balthasar, who is given a letter to Romeo's father and sent away. In fact he hides nearby. Paris is outraged when Romeo begins to open Juliet's tomb. He leaps at Romeo, there is a fight and Paris is killed. Paris's servant runs to fetch help. Romeo opens the tomb, says a last goodbye to Juliet and drinks the poison, falling dead at her side. Friar Laurence and Balthasar now come to the tomb. They find the bodies of Paris and Romeo just as Juliet wakes. The Friar, afraid for his own safety, urges Juliet to leave but she stays behind. Alone, she kills herself with Romeo's dagger.

TOGETHER IN DEATH

Paris's servant has brought help. Balthasar and the Friar have been brought back to the tomb, and the Prince, the Capulets and the Montagues arrive. Friar Laurence tells the tragic story of the young lovers. United by grief the two fathers agree to end their feud and each to have a statue made to commemorate the other's dead child:

*'For never was a story of more woe
Than this of Juliet and her Romeo.'*

The final scene from the 1961 production at the RST. In the tomb, Romeo and Juliet lie together in death, and their families are united in grief.

THE HISTORY OF ROMEO AND JULIET ON STAGE

Places of public assembly, including the theatres, were closed by the Puritans in 1642. There was a gap of nearly twenty years before play-going once more became a part of fashionable London life. The Restoration of the monarchy in 1660 brought back a pleasure-loving Court and a king, Charles II, who loved the arts. *Romeo and Juliet* was one of the first plays to be performed and Samuel Pepys was at the opening night. But as he recorded in his diary, he wasn't too impressed by the performance:

'1662 March 1. To the opera and there saw Romeo and Juliet, the first time it was ever acted, but it is a play of itself the worst that I ever heard in my life, and the worst acted that ever I saw these people do.'

Shakespeare's play was evidently considered too strong to please audiences and an actor-manager, James Howard, presented his own version in which the lovers did not die! There was a period when Shakespeare's play and Howard's play were performed alternately:

'Tragical one Day, and Tragicomical another; for several days together.'

Another version, by Thomas Otway (called *The History and Fall of Caius Marius*), had Juliet waking up before Romeo died. This softening of the ending was kept by the actor David Garrick in his rewriting of the play in 1748. Garrick's version was closer to Shakespeare's but, as well as allowing the lovers to say a tragic goodbye, he also cut out all references to Romeo's early infatuation with Rosaline.

The powerful actor David Garrick, who played Romeo in 1750. He rewrote the play in 1748, cutting out all references to Romeo's early infatuation with Rosaline.

It was not until Sir Henry Irving's production in 1882 that Shakespeare's original version was re-established on the stage. By now leading actors and actresses had realized that success in major roles in this play was the way to stardom.

In 1750 two productions ran in London at the same time with fierce competition for the biggest audience. A critic wrote:

> **'Having seen this play three times at each house... I perceived that Mr Garrick commanded most applause – Mr Barry most tears.'**

Sir Henry Irving's production of *Romeo and Juliet* in 1882 re-established Shakespeare's original version on the stage.

Spranger Barry was the more handsome actor but David Garrick the more powerful:

> **'by a kind of electrical merit Mr Garrick struck all our hearts with a degree of inexpressible feeling.'**

A famous theatrical family of the early nineteenth century, the Kembles, staged a production to give their daughter Fanny the best possible start to her career. Her mother came out of retirement to play Lady Capulet and her father, then over 50, played Mercutio. Their efforts, it was said, 'combined to excite into enthusiasm the assembled audience.'

All the early descriptions of successful Galiots admire an unforced 'natural' style of playing. In large theatres with inadequate lighting, however, there would have been an element of exaggeration we would find unconvincing today. Critics of Henry Irving's performance, with Ellen Terry as Juliet, were disappointed – she was too large and too old:

> **'she is not Juliet... How little Mr Irving is Romeo it is not worth while even to attempt to declare...'**

DIRECTORS' PERSPECTIVES

By the end of the nineteenth century theatre-goers had very strong ideas about what the two lovers should be like. The characters had taken root in the popular imagination. This century the greatest actors and directors have risen to the challenge of the play. Far from wishing to imitate famous productions of the past they have tried to make each new production fresh. There have been some famous experiments: a popular film version directed by Franco Zeffirelli; a highly dramatic ballet, created in 1940, to music by Prokofiev; and, of course, Leonard Bernstein and Stephen Sondheim's 1957 musical, *West Side Story.*

In 1934 the actor-director John Gielgud put together a talented company for a production in which he and Laurence Olivier alternated the parts of **Romeo** and **Mercutio**. Gielgud was brilliant at understanding Shakespeare's language: how to shape a speech and phrase a line to make sense, and to reveal the rhythm and beauty of the poetry. Other actors in the company learned from him and the performance had conviction, pace and energy.

Gielgud was especially successful with the verbal wit of Mercutio while Olivier was more passionate as Romeo. Peggy Ashcroft was praised as 'the finest Juliet of our time'. And as another said of Olivier and Ashcroft as the lovers:

'Larry to me was the Romeo. You got the sex with Larry. They've really got to be in love, these kids.'

John Gielgud's production of the play in 1935. His Mercutio (right) was particularly successful, while Laurence Olivier suited the more passionate Romeo. Edith Evans played the Nurse.

The play has been so frequently performed this century that several leading actors have appeared in more than one production and passed on insights from earlier work. Edith Evans, an outstanding character actress, played the **Nurse** in the 1930s with Ashcroft, Olivier and Gielgud, and again as a very old woman at Stratford upon Avon in 1961. Experience of the world was ingrained in each line of her face, and her extraordinarily flexible, deep voice could still break into a chuckle of pleasure. The director, Peter Hall, used her age and experience as a contrast to a touchingly young Juliet, played by Dorothy Tutin. The bond between them was very strong and made the moment when they no longer felt the same and Juliet is really alone, extremely sad.

In 1976 another young director, Trevor Nunn, assembled a strong cast for his RSC production at Stratford. In the early stages of rehearsal he asked the actors to think back to their own adolescence. They were given homework:

- Do you remember your first adult love-affair or kiss? Jot something down about who, where and maybe what you felt like.

- Write down the most extremely violent thing you have done in your life.

- Jot down a little story about any feud you have known.

This process meant that the actors were using feelings they remembered from their own young lives and their performances were strong and convincing as a result.

Edith Evans played the Nurse in Gielgud's 1935 production of *Romeo and Juliet*, and returned to the role 30 years later under the direction of Peter Hall, with Dorothy Tutin as Juliet. This is taken from the 1961 production at the RST.

Michael Bogdanov has directed *Romeo and Juliet* five times during the last twenty years, and his views on how to make plays written 400 years ago matter now, have developed. One very significant step was the switch to modern dress, which he first used in a performance in 1976. The actors wore costume of the Elizabethan period right up to Juliet's death. Then the last scene, staged as if it were a press conference, called for the unveiling of two gold statues, erected in memory of the two families' dead children. The actors wore modern dress for this scene. Some members of the audience left confused and disgusted at this break with tradition. Others were excited by a final moment which brought the issues of the play right up to date.

Michael Bogdanov's modern-dress production in 1986 had Tybalt (Hugh Quarshie) styled as a leather-clad biker.

Bogdanov explains that with modern dress an audience can pick up information about the characters from what they're wearing, just as we do in ordinary life. For example, the text of the play suggests that **Montague** is of higher social status than **Capulet**. We realize this at a glance if Montague is dressed in an elegant, expensive designer suit and Capulet in a shabby one from a chain store.

In 1989 a production of *Romeo and Juliet* visited a number of towns in Britain. The whole 'kit' – lighting, seating, stage, costumes and so on – was packed up into four 44-foot lorries in one town on a Saturday night and unpacked in another on the Sunday. The staging was set up in a large hall and the production ready for its first audience on

Monday night. Many members of these audiences had seen very few theatre performances before.

The director, Terry Hands, and the designer, Farrah, had clear ideas on what they were aiming for. They wanted to encourage an intimate relationship between what was happening on stage and the people in the audience; they wanted the performance to be powerful and direct. To help this they used a thrust stage, a long rectangular platform with the audience on three sides, so that everyone was close to the action. They kept scenery to a minimum because they didn't want people to be distracted from listening to the vigorous language of the play. They used simple lighting to create atmosphere, including dappled light to suggest moonlight through leaves beneath Juliet's balcony, and just a shaft of light as from a lantern in the darkness of the tomb. The lighting for the daytime street scenes suggested the extreme heat of Italy, and personalities were exaggerated to be in keeping with the Mediterranean climate. The Nurse, for example, positively enjoyed the sexual jokes and teasing and Mercutio was a dangerous, explosive character.

'Shakespeare has put so much into his plays it is like a multi-faceted diamond. Any production team, if they are lucky, might get half of them.'
(Farrah, designer)

Tim McInnerny plays Mercutio in the 1991 RSC production.

ACTORS' PERSPECTIVES

JULIET

Peggy Ashcroft, the **Juliet** of her generation in the 1930s, had this to say about playing Juliet:

'I see Romeo and Juliet as in themselves the most glorious, life-giving people. What you have to take into account is their ages. She is a girl of 14, Romeo is a boy of 16. I discovered in playing her that the essential thing is youth rather than being tragic. I think she's a victim of circumstance. The tragedy is simply something that happens to her.'

Georgina Slowe played Juliet in Terry Hands' 1989 touring production, and the great quality of her performance was youthfulness. She was in her early twenties but, with long dark hair and dressed in simple, flowing costumes, the audience could believe that she was only in her teens. Her quick, light movements and liveliness added even more to this impression.

Peggy Ashcroft, the Juliet of the 1930s, with John Gielgud as Romeo. She saw Juliet as a youthful 'victim of circumstance' rather than a tragic heroine.

In a discussion with a group of students after one performance, Georgina Slowe described the work she had done to find her fourteen-year-old self. She still had diaries she had written at that age and read them again to remind herself of what it felt like to be fourteen.

Claire Holman played Juliet in 1992 in Stratford upon Avon and London. She and her director, David Leveaux, were fascinated by the way **Romeo** talks about her in an almost religious way. She is his 'soul', his good angel, his guiding star.

Any actress playing Juliet is faced by a great acting challenge. She must re-create a young girl who falls deeply in love but is overcome by frighteningly serious problems. Isolated from her family she must face agonizing decisions with extraordinary bravery and sense of purpose. In this 1992 production Claire Holman had to show yet another dimension: the spiritual bond between Juliet and the banished Romeo. The lovers are together only for a very few scenes.

Separated by circumstance, how are they to be together? Here Juliet's balcony was simply a fragile platform suspended high out of reach. The actor playing Romeo

Claire Holman and Michael Maloney in Leveaux's 1992 production. The balcony symbolizes their plight – it is fragile and Romeo has to struggle to reach it.

(Michael Maloney) was given a real physical challenge if he was to reach her. And later in the performance Claire Holman was 'flown in' (suspended high above the stage), to hover over Romeo in Mantua, as if she were a vision inspiring him.

ROMEO

On stage Romeo is often understood most clearly as a contrast to the other young men, particularly **Mercutio**. In Gielgud's production of 1934 (see pages 22 and 23), he and Laurence Olivier alternated the roles, and so understood the difference between them very well.

One of Michael Bogdanov's spectacular modern-dress productions put an Alfa Romeo onto the stage (see page 24), dressed **Tybalt** ('Prince of Cats'), played by Hugh Quarshie, in black biker's leather, while Mercutio (Michael Kitchen) was cool and quietly dangerous. Against this macho world Sean Bean's Romeo was much more open and sensitive, the only one capable of falling in love.

In Terry Hands' 1989 production (see pages 24 and 25), Mark Rylance's Romeo began as a changeable personality, affected by the mood of people around him and beginning to act like them. Mercutio (David O'Hara) was viciously witty, contemptuous of any hint of gentleness or idealism, which he saw as ridiculous. The cynicism of this Mercutio was so extreme that it suggested some hidden pain being covered up. Romeo was responsive to Mercutio's moods and the audience could sense that he understood his friend's deeper feelings. But Romeo here also had an introverted side which led him to spend time alone. When he met Juliet it was as if he had found a soul-mate at last: all his sensitivity and gentleness took over. Juliet rapidly gains the maturity to go her own way and thus Romeo, too, grew up when he fell in love.

The gentle character of Romeo (Olivier, third from right), is often understood in its contrast to the explosive Mercutio (John Gielgud, second from right). This scene is taken from Gielgud's 1935 production.

THE NURSE

Any actress cast as the **Nurse** is presented with a range of choices. She begins as Juliet's closest friend, more of a mother to her than **Lady Capulet**. But while she has a lively personality and can share Juliet's experiences like a friend, she fails to understand the depth of Juliet's feeling for Romeo and lets her down. The actress must think this through in detail, and understand the Nurse's views herself.

When Edith Evans played the Nurse as a very old woman (see page 23) she failed Juliet, inevitably, because of the age gap. The comforting, happy affection between them was something Juliet had to leave behind when she was propelled into adult responsibility. This Nurse couldn't understand Juliet's predicament because the girl's high principles were so very far away from her own priorities for old age. She was looking for security and comfort, for things to stay the same. Inevitably she and Juliet were finally separated by their different perspectives on life.

In 1989 Sheila Reid was a lively, middle-aged Nurse with an earthy zest for life and sex. When she advised Juliet to forget Romeo and marry Paris she showed an eye to the main chance: being true to inner principles meant less to her than securing a good position in the world. (As Juliet's Nurse she would have had a role in the new household.) Sheila Reid managed to make the audience feel that, while she and Juliet had no chance of successfully disobeying the men in authority in their lives, she still regretted that things had to be like that.

Sean Bean and Niamh Cusack in Bogdanov's 1986 production. In contrast with Tybalt's leather and Mercutio's business suit, Romeo's soft outfit emphasized sensitivity and openness.

SHARKS, JETS AND ANIMATED TALES

One of the most successful modern re-creations of *Romeo and Juliet* is the musical *West Side Story*. It was written in 1957 with music by the American composer and conductor, Leonard Bernstein. Lyrics were by Stephen Sondheim, who has gone on to write many other popular musicals. A few years later it was made into a film, directed by Robert Wise and Jerome Robbins. In this version it won the Academy Award for Best Film in 1961.

During the past 30 years the film of *West Side Story* has been seen all around the world. Not only that, the musical has been produced time and again – by professional companies, by amateur groups, and by many schools. Shakespeare's play has come to life for thousands of late twentieth-century school children through the brilliant work of Bernstein and Sondheim and the superb choreography of Jerome Robbins.

They have translated the play and brought it up to date: Verona becomes New York; the Montagues and Capulets are transformed into warring street gangs: the Puerto Rican Sharks against the American Jets. **Juliet** is a Puerto Rican girl, not allowed to mix with mainland boys, but who nevertheless falls in love with one of them.

A modern re-creation of *Romeo and Juliet*, the musical *West Side Story* by Leonard Bernstein. Warring families of medieval Italy are replaced by New York's warring street gangs.

The flood of school productions in the 1960s and '70s encouraged teachers to be bold in exploring Shakespeare in school and to find issues and emotions which are still interesting today. Gradually a more demanding young audience for Shakespeare developed, which in turn encouraged directors like Bogdanov to find exciting ways of communicating.

In fact, the medium of film is helping to create an appetite for Shakespeare in even younger children. In 1993 six of the plays became 'animated tales' for television. Each one used a different technique of animation and *Romeo and Juliet* was shown as a romantic fairy-tale looking rather like a classic Disney cartoon.

In this retelling of the story great emphasis was placed on the beauty of the medieval Italian setting and on the blossoming of young love. Like all the animated tales, Shakespeare's play was reduced to only twenty minutes. However, the essence of the story was successfully captured in Leon Garfield's version and it is already proving a good introduction to the play for a wide range of people.

In the nineteenth century there often seemed to be an ideal, and rather sentimental, picture of *Romeo and Juliet*, against which all actual productions were measured.

Twentieth-century actors, directors, and those who have re-created the play in a new medium, have brought to light the toughness of the play. They have shown that young love must make hard decisions, and that all too often it is doomed by the violence of society. The tragedy of **Romeo** and Juliet is also the tragedy of the Montagues and the Capulets. It is the tragedy of any divided, violent society – including ours today.

Romeo and Juliet shows us what damage divided and violent societies can have on individual lives. This scene is taken from the 1976 production at The Other Place, in Stratford upon Avon.

INDEX